Monochrome

A Canvas of Poetry

Shagufta Siddiqa

BookLeaf Publishing

India | USA | UK

*To all of them who need poetry and also who
think they don't...*

Acknowledgements

I owe my deepest gratitude to the poets whose words have left an indelible mark on my soul, resonating with each layer of meaning they unveil. To Rabindranath Tagore, Shakti Chattopadhyay, Nirendranath Chakravarty, Sylvia Plath, John Berger, Pablo Neruda, Emily Dickinson, Jorge Luis Borges, Federico García Lorca and so many others – thank you for illuminating the beauty of words and feeling.

My heartfelt thanks also go to my family, especially Maa and Papa, whose unwavering support has been my strength, and to the dear friends who have encouraged me to share my voice and bring this book into being. This journey holds special meaning, as my late grandfather Prof. Fakhruddin Siddiqi Asar was also a poet. It brings me immense joy to honour his art and celebrate the timeless connections that poetry fosters among us.

I find a strange and quiet power in the darker days of life. The broken canvas of life made of 'grey crayon' has been crucial in all my writings. I hope we each hold onto our unique 'crayon' to paint oceans and rainbows even when the time is not right, in fact, especially if the time is not right.

Finally, I extend my gratitude to my publisher for believing in this collection and providing me the opportunity to share it with others.

Preface

Poetry is the portrait of musings and reflection of our soul. Somehow, it manages to hit the finest chord of our hearts. This book reveals a collection of abstract poems through a monochromatic lens. May we find ourselves in order to lose it again in our wildest dreams and striking connotations and still have the courage to reignite our heart to find ourselves in this amazing journey of life; that's all about poetry, and it talks about our very own reality, which we create.

Monochrome

A thematic show staged in a perfect row;
A furious crowd found it socially loud.

A better deal would have been an empty house;
Hundred years ago, there was also a lonely
leaning couch.

A woman's dance with twisted ankles;
She broke out of her own early shackles.

A heaven made of cruel lies;
A humanity justifying social cries.

A race against the wind was won;
A lover boy felt his time was gone.

And it was the abstract art of the game;
It was the bloody trick of a broken frame.

They let the history repeat itself;
As learning from it was safely parked on a shelf.

In the dungeon of hues, it was the end
Love was inherently an easy spend.

To the mighty self of truth and dare;
It was all about to sleep in despair.

Colours were blended into one perfect shade
Monochrome too was about to fade!

Water is Contaminated

Striking through the invisible lines, it's a story of
a story;
Chasing the dreamy eyes, it's a race against the
racer;
Flying around the war track, it's a revelation of
the revolution.

I see my tears forming a storm of the north,
I see my blood flowing in the nearby river,
I see my scar turning into a red moon,
I see my burning body hanging from the magical
sky.
I see, and I crave for water…
Perhaps here the water is contaminated.

Magnus & Myth

An Art and the Architecture;
The Victory and the Valour;
The Class and the Crown;
The Magnus and the Myth;
The Kingdom and the Kind;
History carefully wipes the mind.

Dress code of Sanity

Crash my party and hold my hand,
Dance to the tune on the whimsy sand.

Put up a mask and lit up a glass,
Violet sky has the purple grass.

For that, this myst is the new smoke;
For that, in smoke, I become you;
For that, you dissolve in vanity;
And now this vanity is the dress code of sanity!

Lab No. 9

Created by a magic spell, it was a garden of
flowers;
Delighted in cosy affair, lonely winter was kept
in the wooden drawers.

In early days of spring, it was a glitch of a fancy
string;
The black guitar was now a memoir of a
wedding ring.

A smile relinquished its crown of love to the
ashes of snow;
It was a river that decided not again to flow.

A season passed, a lifetime lost
The mountain of pain was never crossed.

I waited and waited, I sang our love songs where
the heart was wronged;
I thought and thought and buried myself in a
hidden crest where it belonged.

Yes, I was convicted of a felony…
I chose to take a leap from the fifth-floor
balcony.

I lost the battle of every day to win a moment–
A moment of hope that was free from torment–
A torment of a dark tide that wiped a tent–
A tent of our little nest and a future we dreamt…
A dream of poems with blood-red paint.

A paint of blood, a leap of mine,
A death of a skeleton, lab no. 9.

(put) A STOP

A sinking ship got trapped in the dead sea...
A bloodbath of heart was intact in a cup of tea...

A ship, a spring and two bodies–
They all lost the battle.

A poetry of musings
A portrait of flashbacks
A symphony of chaos
A horizon of smoke
A cemetery of dreams
An end of endings
A bit of this and rest of that...
Finally came to a stop.

A Wake-up Story

I wake up to a morning of white snow.
I somehow end up sitting at your last show.

I move to a bookstore with a fancy crowd of
readers;
I somehow get into an ugly sequence of desires.

I take the next right turn at the end of the hill;
I look at the soldiers busy with a fake drill.

I see through a mirror of scratchy faces;
I choose to be comfortably naive in dark places.

I hold my coffee mug and a dewdrop on a silver
saucer;
I often become the crafted protagonist of the
failed author.

Is it a sign of outrageous felony of an outcasted
mind?
Well, I somehow reach there to unwind.

I somehow wake up to something.

Skin

Tied to the body and far from the soul;
It was a myth that I wasn't even part of the
whole.

Riding to the bottom of the lane and keeping the
promises aside;
It was a myth that it was less than a heart's
homicide.

Stabbing to death and not being able to die;
It was a myth that lie was all about happy high...

Burning me upside down and making it a huge
win;
It was a myth that it was only my skin.

I still carry the skin; I carry the mere skin.

Here Again

May the lilac bloom in this garden,
May the girl now find a lost kite back in the den.
May this time she look at the valley of mayhem;
May her soul rest in peace here again.

Golden Sky

Rhythm of a romantic tune lost its way to the
massive wound;
Into the wild forest of pines, a dead poet was
found.

Inhibiting the truth and glorifying the dare;
It was a broken stiletto and the easy chair...

Disappearing poems of a vandalised notebook;
It was a story of a mortal chess and its helpless
rook.

In the glory of the utmost guilt and sly;
I miss my bird in the golden sky.

I See You

At every late-night party, I see you sitting at the
corner table with a flat white latte.
I see you, and I deny you.

In every monsoon, I see you watching me play
with a paper boat from a distance.
I see you, and I deny you.

In every street of Kolkata, I see you smashing
zillions of queues with your charming hues.
I see you, and I keep on seeing you.
Over and over again.

Bury My Red Sea

Unwritten poems of a dead sea turned into
Undeniable truth of a falling star,
Uninterrupted chaos of a screaming heart,
Unwatchable scenes of a battlefield,
Unforgiven and truly unfair deal of love.
That's all needed to unlove and bury that dead
blood sea in the poem of love!

Miracle

She who doesn't believe in the lost quotes of a
madman's diary,
She who doesn't dance anymore with her
chronic fury.
She who still lives in the hotel, room no. 109,
She who has violated the mocking rules, nearly
borderline.
In her static law of monumental misconduct,
It was a crime thriller of her ultimate
reconstruct.
It was a song of spring and the cry of monsoon...
It was a dance of Satan and the mourning moon.
It was an eclipse of a blood-red sky,
It was the miracle of a blatant lie!

Fossil of Heart

A fossil here is resting in peace now;
Reaching to death is just the beginning of the
vow.

Witnessing the tough wind of a forgotten winter;
The sky has come here... to hold the white cloak,
To mend the wounds;
To stitch the ripped skin;
To create a fountain spring in the heart;
But here the cold has a magic spell,
The sky is now just a lost rebel.

Here, death is the queen with her white
neckpiece,
Indeed, fossil of heart is resting in peace.

Emerge in Love

By the shadow of death, you were a crystal
mirage...
Indebted in shallow dignity, you did emerge.
You emerged in lie;
You emerged in breaking the last piece of hope;
You emerged to horrify the heart to the core;
You emerged to destroy the idea of justice;
You emerged in your kind of truth, which lacked
stability;
Your emergence was a manifestation of a
betrayal...
You emerged in this and that;
You emerged so that love might not emerge at
all.

Silver Tree

Reckoning with the radiant dark web;
Imposter has missed that very step.

Into the shady form of dreamy desires;
The whole forest suddenly disappears.

But then touching a silver tree and weeping in
glee–
It is the sign of a soothing soul to flee.

Writing a mammoth list for the 100th time;
Nope, it is not worth calling a dime.

So where does the soul take a nap?
Exactly where it gets a happy snap!

And Then…

19

It takes a blink of an eye
It appears to be a deep breath of sigh.

It takes a whole life and still remains in store
It breaks the heart every time a little more.

But then it is what the heart longs for
And then the soul never returned to where it was
before!

A Poisonous Heart

Burning his songs and pouring into the glass of
wine;
A drop of that wine melting the fine silk of his
hope;
The last piece of hope he brought with a ripped
photograph;
It was a deal between the screaming mind of his
and the poisonous heart of hers;
It was a deal of a million shiny stars and a black
little spot.
It was me with a heart.
It was me with the poisonous heart.

Null

Through the cracking window, my skull fell;
It fell and fell apart.
Through the burning walls, my skin to pay;
It was a pay for a payback.
Through the bloodshed of poetry, my void
became null;
It was nullified, insatiably nullified.

Afterglow

The moment of despair in that tricky affair,
The relentless storm of the forgotten summer...
Barged into the room of the magician.
'So it was the end': a note in a red crayon;
Flew across the horizon and beyond...
It was a bird with no wings;
And also a kite with no strings.
It was a volcano in the sky;
And also a calm sea of golden dye.
It was the beginning of another anecdote with a
shining glow;
And also millions of years ago, we called it our
afterglow!

A Celestial Coral

In the vanity of wishes, you are the finest piece
of art.
Breaking into my house of forgotten shadows,
you accepted the broken heart.

In the vast sanity of Marine Drive, you are the
mark of the sea;
In the long drive to Mysuru, you are a date over
a cup of tea.

On a dizzy day with a tizzy mind, you are the
vicious tranquillizer.
And again, in the stormy woods, you are the lost
fragrance of the breezy air.

In a heart of junk desires, you are my part of
self-diligence;
Delving into the blue ocean, you are the wave of
magnificence.

Despite the vehemence against the fleeting
moments, you've become a lifetime,
It is that time of the year, a soul chooses to
vanish every other time.

In my wild imagination, if you watch me there
to fly high;
In the world of our own, you are my celestial
coral of 3rd July!

Passerby

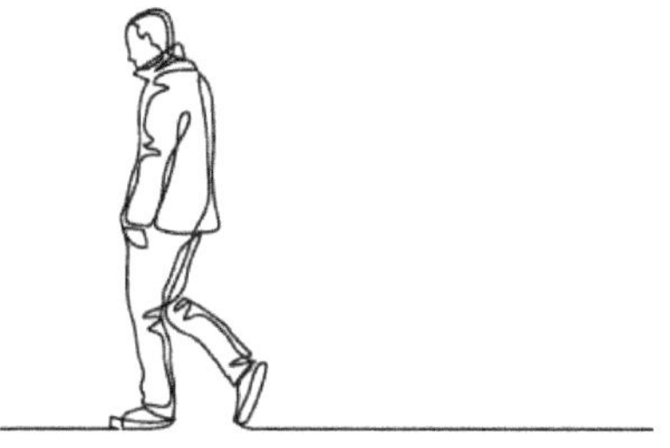

In an evening of weary summer
It is the soothing breeze of the lost monsoon
Which carries along the tiddly soul,
Which brings back the windy rain,
Which plays around the City of Joy,
Which recalls the wuthering waves of broken...
mind which stays in the stealing gaze of
passerby!

A Lavender and The Soldier

A sunflower garden and a hazy frontier;
She was a soft lavender to the eye of a soldier…
A red sky and a rocket with an exposure,
The bloodbath was an amusing roller coaster.
The silent world with a bunch of clowns,
Leading the throne of ghost towns!
A coin tossed and a fate flopped,
A rusted sword and the truth was chopped.
She was a lavender to the eye of the soldier;
Till it was smashed to dust in early October.

Genocide

If it's not a genocide, it's a war for you;
If it's not a child, it's a collateral damage for
you.
If it's still a slice of Gaza and not your
comfortable hypocrisy,
You do belong to a side, a side of annihilating
theocracy!

Memoir

To a journey that is a forever story and more,
To the phoenix who is born again with a roar;
To the apocalypse that is lost by the shore.
To this life only to adore!